LIBRARY, REGISTRATION & INFORMATION SERVICES
Please return/renew item by last date shown - thank you for using your library

100 ways to keep your baby smiling

12-18 months

Ideas 63-100

including: • kitchen fun, and
meuletime tips and treats
• puzzles • farm animals and
animal rhymes • going to the
seaside • doing a workout
• playing footie • going
swimming • bathtime fun

Further information on
Tommy's Campaign

Acknowledgments

Dorling Kindersley

LONDON, NEW YORK, SYDNEY, DELHI,
PARIS, MUNICH and JOHANNESBURG

Senior Managing Art Editor Lynne Brown

Senior Managing Editor Corinne Roberts

Art Editor Glenda Fisher

Project Editor Valerie Kitchenham

DTP Designer Rajen Shah

Production Joanna Bull

First published in Great Britain in 2000
by Dorling Kindersley Limited,
9 Henrietta Street, Covent Garden,
London WC2E 8PS

ISBN 0 7513 0711 4

Reproduced by Colourscan, Singapore.
Printed and bound by
South China Printing Co. Ltd

see our complete catalogue at
www.dk.com

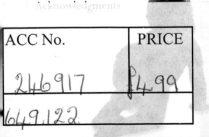

Introduction

Every day, thousands of people experience the thrill of becoming parents to a healthy baby who will bring them no end of joy. And for those parents, a primary concern will be to ensure that their baby remains healthy, happy and stimulated, nurtured by an environment that offers limitless opportunities for development through learning and play. This is where *The Happy Baby Book* can help. Packed with 100 ideas for keeping a baby amused, it is designed to inspire parents, grandparents, aunties, uncles and carers alike.

Sadly, however, not everyone is fortunate enough to experience the joy of having a happy, healthy baby and the sorrow and heartache felt at the loss of a tiny life is indescribable. This is where **Tommy's Campaign** – a national charity funding medical research into the causes of stillbirth, premature birth and miscarriage – has a vital role to contribute. The charity also provides helpful information and literature for parents and for those who are thinking about starting a family.

The single aim of **Tommy's Campaign** is to give babies a better start in life by making pregnancy and birth healthier and safer for baby and mother. It's astounding to learn that every year in the UK alone:

- 1 in 5 pregnancies ends in miscarriage
- 1 in 188 babies is tragically lost through stillbirth
- 100 babies a day are born too small or too soon.

It is also sobering to realise that these figures haven't really changed since the 1930's, so the need for medical research remains as urgent as ever. **Tommy's Campaign** receives no government funding, which means that without your generosity the charity would not be able to support the research projects that are needed throughout the UK. For every copy sold of *The Happy Baby Book*, 13p will go to **Tommy's Campaign**.

Thank you for your support in helping to give every baby the best possible start in life.

Finding the answers to problem pregnancies

Registered charity number 1060508

For information on **Tommy's Campaign**, you can call 020 7620 0188 or write to: Tommy's Campaign, Freepost (Lon 1053), London SE99 6RD. Using a stamp will save the charity money. For details on how to join 'smalltalk', Tommy's Campaign's new club for parents, just turn to the back of this book.

birth - 3 months

THE FIRST THREE MONTHS are an exciting time for you
and your baby as you both get to know one another. You'll be
thrilled and intrigued as you watch him gradually learn to
smile, follow things with his eyes, respond to sounds and
coo with pleasure. At this stage, the key to ensuring
your baby's contentment is simply to make him feel loved and
secure in his amazing new world. The following 15 ideas
will make him feel safe and happy through the reassuring
sensations of touch, sight and sound – what better
start in life could you give him?

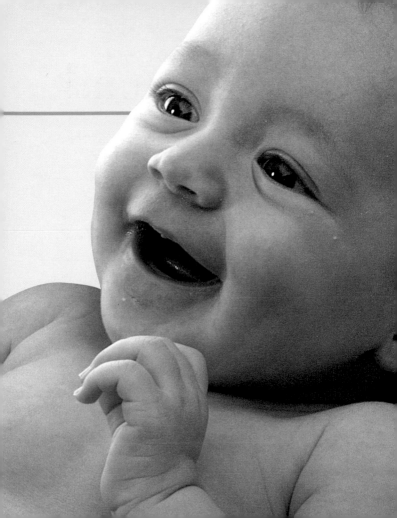

1

talk to her

Your new baby will love to hear you talk. She'll recognise the rhythms from when she was in the womb, so your voices will be a familiar link with the world she's emerged into.

2

smile at her

Keep smiling! Your baby will look very comical as she starts to copy your various facial expressions.

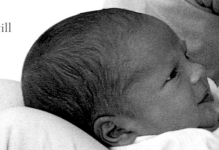

3

sing a lullaby

A baby is born with rhythm. She picks it up from hearing her mother's heartbeat while in the womb and from experiencing the rocking sensation of her walk as she is carried around in her pelvis for nine months. So the sound of a caring voice singing a lilting, rhythmical song is the perfect soother for when she needs calming. If you've forgotten the words of childhood nursery rhymes and lullabies, you can always sing a familiar television programme theme tune or any song that your baby hears often. You will find yourself swaying naturally as you sing.

4

keep him cosy

Your baby has no in-built temperature control, so you have to make sure he doesn't get too cold, nor too warm. Lay him on a warm towel to change him.

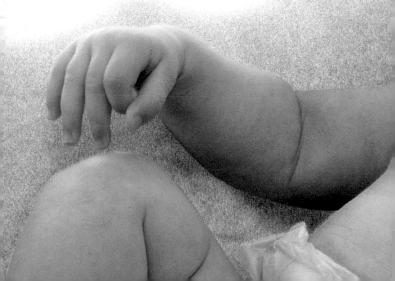

5

make her feel safe

A new baby has new skin, so wrap her in soft, natural materials as she will enjoy their comforting texture. Being wrapped or swaddled makes her feel safe – having spent nine months in a confined space, the big wide world can seem frightening to a tiny baby. Many newborns dislike being naked, so if she seems unsettled at changing times try draping a muslin cloth or nappy over her tummy as this may make her feel happier and less exposed.

cuddle up close

A baby can be wrapped up as snug as a bug, but there's no substitute for cuddling up to mum. Just lying together for a rest or a feed is enough for your baby to feel blissfully secure. You can relax, too, and revel in watching him snooze or suckle.

7

give him a mobile

Your newborn can see up to 20–25cm (8–10in) away and by three months he may be able to focus on a mobile. Hang one over his cot and its colourful shapes will delight him. Ensure the mobile is out of reach if you leave him alone with it.

8

put rings on her wrist...

Bees, butterflies and bunnies – there are all manner of fun
wrist rattles available for your baby to get her hands on. Give
her one to play with and watch her face light up.

9

and bells on her toes!

Help your baby to find her feet by sewing bells on her socks, but do make sure they're still attached very securely before you put them on each time. She will love to hear them tinkle.

10

let teddy take over...

...so you can have a break from providing the entertainment. Nothing beats the timeless child appeal of a big soft teddy bear – babies find their faces fascinating. Make sure any cuddly toy you give your child complies with all current safety standards.

11

bring in
big brother

Babies find children intriguing, so let an older brother or
sister (or a friendly tame toddler!) have a go at entertaining.
But never leave an older child alone with a baby.

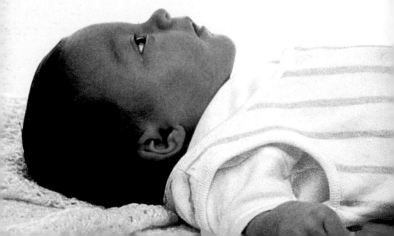

Get out and about with...

...a carrier

This is a nifty solution for
transporting your baby, both
in and out of the car. Some
designs fit onto accompanying
buggy/pushchair frames, too,
for added versatility.

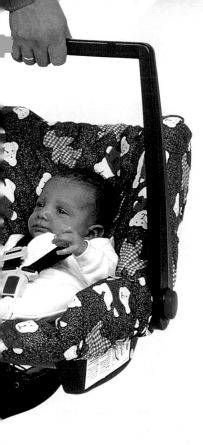

13

...a buggy

Just getting fresh air and
meeting a friend will change
the mood of a fractious day.
Get out for a walk with the
buggy or pram – prop up your
baby so she can look around.

14

...a sling

A sling is a very handy
means of transport, as it
offers your baby comforting
body contact and allows you
to carry her while leaving
your hands free.

re

laaaax

3 - 6 months

DURING THESE MONTHS you'll notice your baby becoming more sociable as she burbles and chuckles and takes greater notice of people around her. She'll study things closely as her focusing improves and everything she touches will end up in her mouth as she explores texture and taste. This is a fun time as she gains the strength to roll from her back to her front and push herself up. The next 19 ideas will all encourage her to learn about her body and what it can do – from playing with her toes to splashing in water, enjoying new tastes to bopping in a baby bouncer.

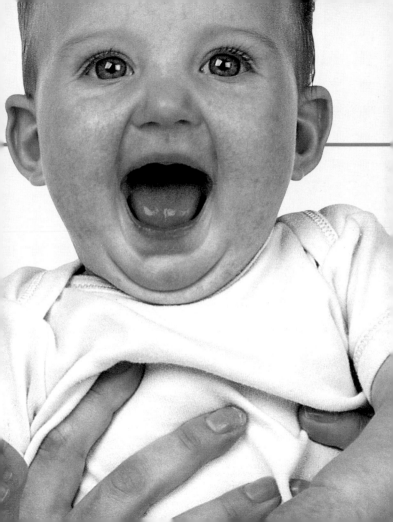

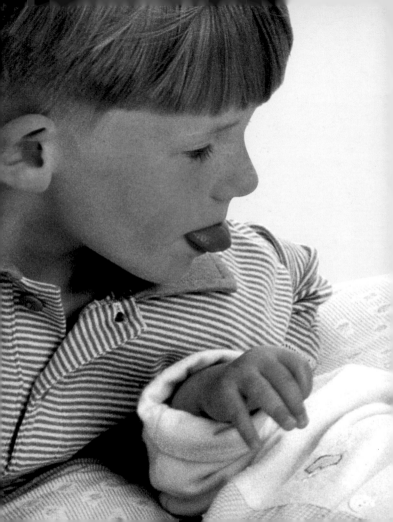

16

blow a raspberry!

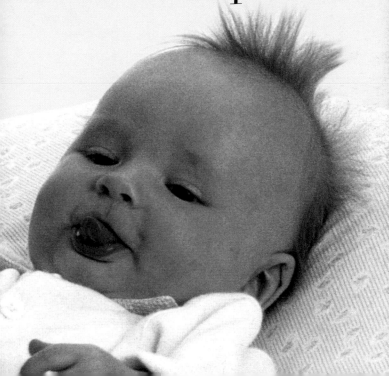

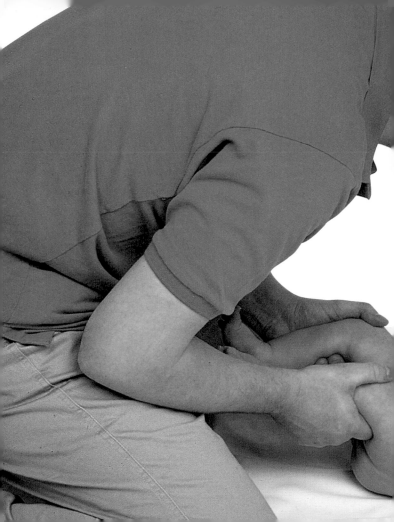

let him kick

As any pregnant mum knows, babies love to kick – it's an early form of exercise. Let yours kick, nappy-free, during changes. It will keep rashes at bay by getting air to that bottom, too.

18

"massage me!"

Nothing is more soothing than a gentle all-over massage – it's the natural way to establish a bond with your baby through touch. First, make sure the room is warm and your baby is content, then lay him on a thick towel. Working downwards from shoulders to feet, lightly move your hands over his body, using a little baby oil to soften his skin. Talk or sing to him as you go, or play relaxing music in the background.

19

"tickle me!"

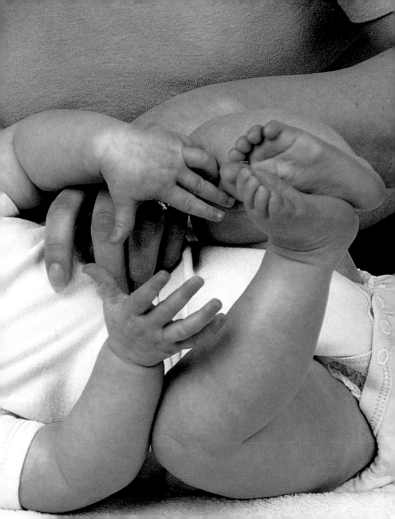

20

play with her fingers...

Your baby will soon begin to explore her own hands and
fingers and you can join in with these discoveries by singing
hand-action rhymes with her. A fun rhyme to sing is *One,
two, three, four, five / Once I caught a fish alive...*

21

play with her toes...

Her toes are a source of wriggly fascination for
your baby. By gently touching each toe in turn, you
can stimulate her range of sensations — and guarantee
getting a giggle! Try playing *This little pig went to market*
while she is lying down having her nappy changed
or when she is snuggled up close on your knee.

...this little piggy...

...let her have a go!

Gotcha! Once your baby knows they're there, her hands and toes will become her favourite playthings. Give her the freedom to get to know her own body — it will contribute to her developing sense of self-awareness. By grabbing her toes, she is experimenting with hand-eye co-ordination and starting to understand perspective.

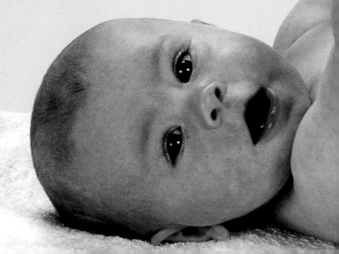

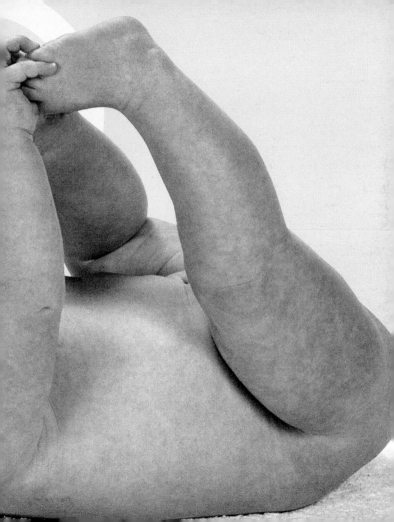

Show him the world...

23 ...from a ringside seat

Once your baby can hold his head up – maybe from as early
as six weeks – you can pop him in a baby chair. This will
make him feel more involved in what's going on. Never put
the chair on a table or leave him unattended while he's in it.

24 ...in a mirror

Let him look in a mirror and talk to him about the little boy
he can see there. He will be intrigued by the puzzled face that
is peering back at him.

25 ...from up high and all around

With a bouncer, your baby can spin himself around and bop
up and down. He'll be thrilled by the freedom it offers him to
see the world from an upright position.

26

give him some space

As your baby approaches six months, he may be able to sit propped up by cushions. Encourage him to have a go – you'll find he loves the sense of freedom it gives him. Put his favourite toys in front of him, sit back and give him some space to enjoy playing by himself. It's important he learns to enjoy periods of quieter, more introspective play so that you can intersperse these with more energetic forms of activity as he gets older. This way he'll learn to enjoy his own company as well as that of others.

Make mealtimes scrummy

27

...puréeing

To purée, push cooked fruit
or veg through a sieve.

28

...steaming

This maintains nutrients –
most vegetables steam well.

29

...poaching

Cook in a little water to
poach both fruit and veg.

and textures yummy by...

30
...mashing

Bananas mash beautifully,
but so do juicy mangoes.

31
...blending

Be daring – blend flavours,
such as apple and pear.

32
...combining

Combine textures, such as
baby rice with courgette.

33

As soon as your baby can grab and hold an object, she'll enjoy some simple bathtime toys. Bright yellow ducks are firm favourites, especially if they come in families. She can play with one, while the others bob about around her.

go quackers!

34

have a happy
water baby

Your baby may love her bath, but hair-washing is often another
matter entirely. Many babies dislike water and bubbles running
into their eyes, so minimize bathtime tears by gently sponging
water onto her head rather than allowing it to trickle down
onto her face. Alternatively, you could buy a shampoo guard —
this is designed to shield the eyes from soapy dribbles.

6-12 months

AT THIS STAGE in his development, your little
one goes from barely being able to sit up to
taking his first few faltering steps. By his first
birthday you'll wonder where your little baby has
gone! This is a time of rapid progress as your
child's hearing, co-ordination and spatial
awareness become increasingly sophisticated and
his growing strength and balance allow him to
learn to sit alone, crawl and pull himself up to
cruise around the furniture. Now it is variety
that's the key to keeping your child happy and
stimulated – turn the page for more clever ideas
that are guaranteed to keep him smiling…

35

send in a granny

Any granny (or grandad!) will do the trick – they are all past masters in the art of baby entertainment and know no end of rhymes, games and pacifying techniques that are guaranteed to work. What they can offer your baby is different to what you can offer, and that's the secret of their success – after all, variety is the spice of life, even when you're six months old.

help him sleep easy

An older baby doesn't automatically doze off in your arms after a feed, so you can no longer expect to put him in his cot already asleep. To ensure happy bedtimes, he needs to get used to going to bed while he is awake and learn to get off to sleep alone without getting anxious. You can help by making his cot an interesting place to be with toys and a mobile (out of reach when he's alone with it). This will help when he wakes in the morning too, as he may play for a while before calling you.

37

"go, baby, go!"

Once your baby is mobile there's
no stopping her, so baby-proof your
home and create a safe area where she
will be able to explore freely. She needs
watching, but you'll be more relaxed if
you reduce the hazards. If you want to
keep her 'captive' for a while, use a
mesh-sided playpen.

give him something
safe to...

...throw

...chew

...stack

39
play
peek-a-

bOO

give him a box!

It's an old joke among parents, but babies often do seem to prefer the box to the gift inside it. So, forget the new toy, just give your baby an empty box (without staples or sharp edges) and he'll be happy.

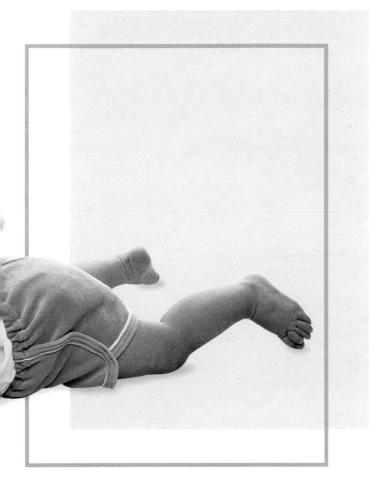

41

sing...

Row, row, row
your boat,

gently down the
stream,

merrily, merrily,
merrily, merrily,

life is but a
dream.

play in the sand

Sifting, moulding and mixing
sand will keep your baby
busy. Always fit a lid on the
pit, so the sand stays clean.

Go into the garden and...

43

dig in a
flower pot

44

roll on
the grass

45

listen for birds

46

smell the flowers...

Take your baby into the garden or to the park to show him the flowers. Talk to him about their bright colours and let him smell them and handle their petals. He'll be intrigued by their fragrance and velvety texture. Although they might look good enough to eat, make sure none ends up in his mouth.

47

...and feel the leaves

Pick leaves for him to handle and scrunch up, and tickle his nose with blades of grass. Early experiences like this are important as a means of introducing him to nature and the world around him.

Rock 'n' roll

48
let him jingle
some bells...

50
shake some
maracas...

49
bash on a
xylophone...

51
bang a toy
drum or...

52

...a saucepan!

Give her a pan to bash with a wooden spoon. She'll love to hear the satisfying 'dong'.

53

click spoons

She can click wooden spoons together or 'play' the fridge door. You have been warned!

54

make a shaker

Take a small plastic bottle and pour in some dry rice. Ensure the top is securely tightened.

55

listen to notes

Fill empty plastic bottles with varying levels of water. Blow over the top of each. Listen...

56 play...

...pointing games together. Once your baby can point, she's found a new way of communicating. Now she can tell you what she wants and where she wants to go without saying a word.

where's the

give grandad a call

58

give him
a biscuit

Get gums chewing and new teeth nibbling with healthy snacks. If his tummy is rumbling, finger foods will fill the gap. Try a stick of cheese or carrot, or chopped seedless grapes and slices of banana. The occasional plain biscuit is good, too. Always watch while he eats in case anything goes down the wrong way.

59

...or let him get stuck in!

60

"give her a hug"

Make your baby happy by booking up a busy social life
with little friends. Ensure success by keeping visits to
playmates short but sweet, so there's no time for tears.

61

use up
some
energy

There's nothing more exhilarating than the
sensation of being whisked through the air.
Your baby will thrill to some safe, controlled
rough and tumble — but don't overdo it.

62
enjoy books

A book is amazing. It opens and closes, has colourful pictures and words that make stories and, if it's a board book, your baby can chew it and drop it, and it will still be fun to look at.

12 - 18 months

THIS IS THE TIME of walking and talking and you'll find your child goes up a gear and wants to be into everything. As well as experimenting with his first real steps and first real words, he will be fascinated by books and scribbling and will enjoy feeding himself at mealtimes. And, as his balance and confidence grow, he'll become more sure-footed and will soon be charging about, busying himself in a world of pretend play, copying your behaviour and conversational chit-chat. To prevent boredom, let him enjoy his growing independence – the following ideas offer some useful ways of keeping him interested and amused.

buy him a spare snuggle bunny

If your baby has formed an attachment with one particular toy, the chances are he'll love it so hard that it will end up looking nothing like the teddy or baa-lamb it once was. A clever tip is to buy a spare – an identical 'snuggle bunny' or 'cuddly' that you can substitute once the original has seen better days or interchange with the other to make both last longer.

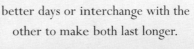

64 ...a lift-out game

Fitting the right shape in the right hole can be quite difficult, so your child will need your help to begin with.

65 ...a giant jigsaw

Go for specially designed big-piece jigsaw puzzles. They will help to develop hand-eye co-ordination.

66 ...a shape-sorter

This toy requires your child to post 3-D shapes through their corresponding window and encourages shape-matching skills.

67 ...pairing cards

A card game involving matching up identical images of animals, for example, has a simple appeal. Always give lots of praise.

Set him a puzzle

challenge with...

Tiny hands can...

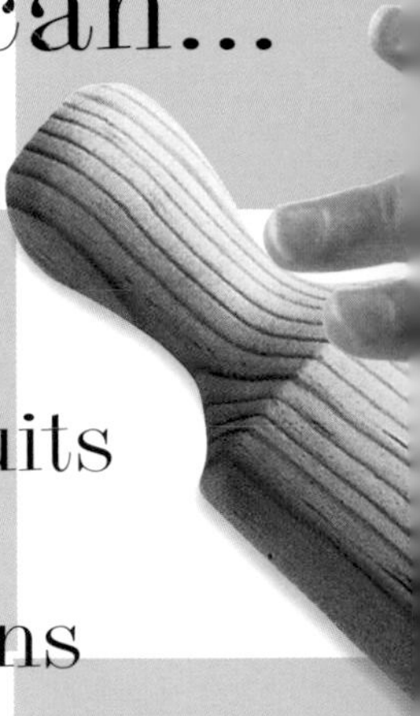

68 roll pastry

69 decorate biscuits

70 stack saucepans

71 help lay place mats

72 put fruit in the bowl

73 help unpack shopping

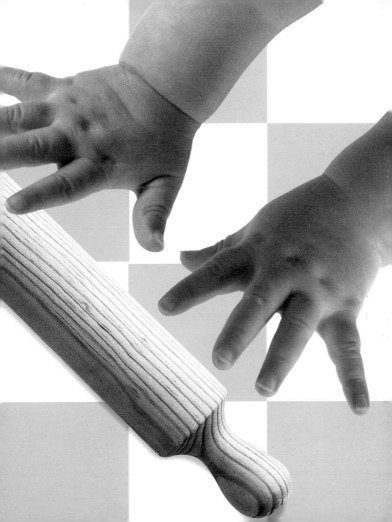

74

make mealtimes

Bring your baby to the table and make eating a sociable affair.
Put the highchair away and use a booster seat for family
meals. Give him his own cutlery
and introduce new tastes.

lots of fun...

...with fabulous fish

Babies can be fickle eaters, so it pays to be inventive when introducing new tastes. If you find it hard to tempt your child at mealtimes, try experimenting with the way in which you present her food. Why not be inspired by this fishy dish (flaked fish spooned inside a yellow-pepper outline) to make

make a tasty

all sorts of appetizing treats to tempt your child? Think about how you might use nutritious staples, such as fruit, vegetables, bread and pasta to create fun food animals or comical faces on her plate. She'll probably enjoy eating her peas and carrots if she thinks she's eating a scary monster's eyes and nose!

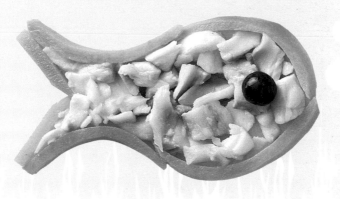

ocean dish

...and busy bees

Bees, butterflies, beetles and spiders – there are all
sorts of nice things and nasties you can serve up as dessert!
Take ice-cream, jelly or blancmange, and get creative...

make creepy

take some ice-cream...

Take a scoop of ice-cream and place in a shallow
dish. Decorate with chocolate-chip eyes, liquorice legs, wafer
wings – whatever you fancy to create your creepy-crawly.

wobbly jelly...

Make up jelly according to packet instructions. Pour into
small individual jelly moulds to set. Use a cake-decorator's
icing bag to pipe on cream spots, wings or spindly legs.

or creamy blancmange!

Make up blancmange according to packet instructions. Pour
into moulds, leave to set, turn out, then decorate to make
your creepy-crawly. Sit on a bed of lime jelly 'grass', if desired.

crawly treats

Talk about farm

77

...look at farmyard books

baaa

78

...make animal noises

79

...make a toy farm

animals and...

moO

cluck
cluck

Sing animal rhymes!

80

hickory dickory dock

Hickory dickory dock,
the mouse ran up the clock.
The clock struck one,
the mouse ran down,
hickory dickory
dock.

81

incy-wincy spider

Incy-wincy spider climbed up the water spout,
down came the raindrops and washed poor Incy out.
Out came the sunshine and dried up all the rain,
Incy-wincy spider climbed up the spout again.

82

two little dicky birds

Two little dicky birds sitting on a wall,
one named Peter, one named Paul.
Fly away Peter! Fly away Paul!
Come back Peter, come back Paul.

Go to the seaside

83

...have
a paddle

84

...build a
sandcastle

and...

85

...make footprints
in the sand

86

...dig a pool

87

...collect shells

88

"go down under"

Share your baby's perspective on things by getting down
to her level and crawling around with her. Let her see
how things look upside down by showing her how to peep
through her own legs — she'll find it highly amusing.

89

"fly way up high"

Encourage your baby to get a new angle on the world by
lifting her up high or onto your shoulders (mind her head!).
This will give her a bird's-eye view of proceedings and will
help to develop her sense of spatial awareness.

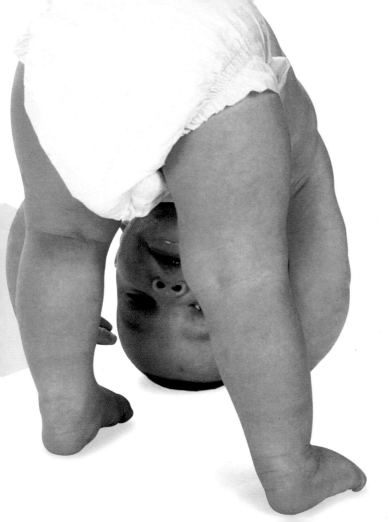

Do a workout

gently lift and rock

Once your baby is walking and his neck and back
muscles are stronger, you can try new rough and
tumble games, like this one. Tip your baby onto the
soles of your feet, hold onto his arms and rock him
backwards and forwards in the air. When he's bigger
do the same thing, but support him on your shins.

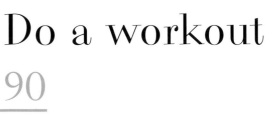

touch your toes

This might be easier for
him than for you!

stretch your arms

Stand with feet apart and arms outstretched.
Lift your arms to the side to play 'aeroplanes'.

stretch your legs

Lie down on your back and swing one leg
over the other. See if your baby can do it too.

94

have a game
of footie

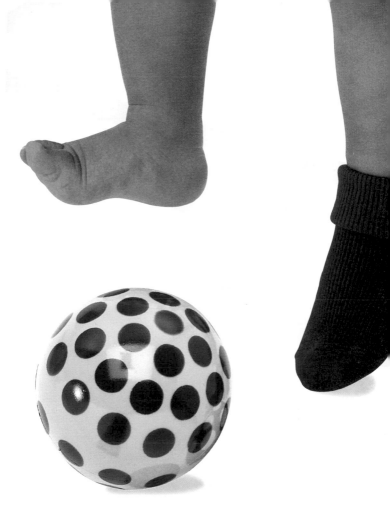

Make bathtime fun

95
...bubbles

97
...scooping
and pouring

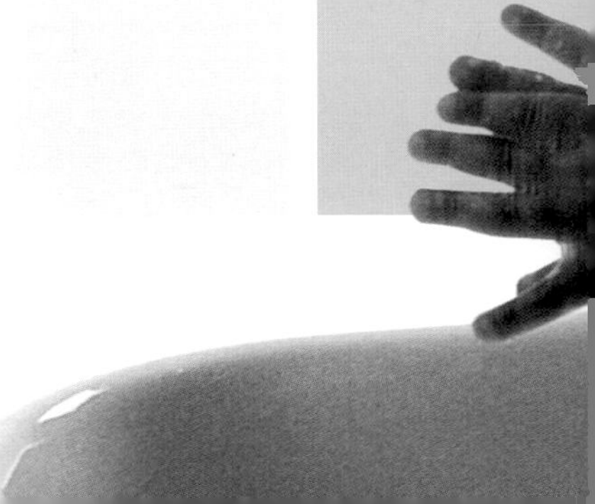

96
...splashing and squirting

with...

98

go for a swim

Your baby will love the sensation of floating in a swimming pool from an early age – many young babies are more mobile in water than on dry land. You can take her to lessons or just regular sessions in the 'baby' pool. She'll enjoy the swim and after, thanks to the exercise, she'll be relaxed and happy.

99

let him dry himself...

As part of your older baby's developing independence, make time for some DIY care! Start bathtime a little earlier and then let him dry himself and try to put on his pyjamas, with as little help from you as possible. This is good fun for him and may well cut down on a lot of wriggling and complaining.

100

let him loose!

Young toddlers are exuberant about their bodies
and sometimes clothes can feel a little constricting.
They much prefer to show off their birthday suits,
loving the sensation of bare skin and running
around with absolutely nothing on. So, after a bath,
or when it's warm and sunny outside, let your child
express himself with all his natural enthusiasm!

Celebrate the birth of a baby

What is Tommy's Campaign?

Tommy's Campaign is the only UK charity focusing exclusively on healthy pregnancies and babies. Our aim is to give babies the very best start in life by funding pioneering research into premature birth, stillbirth and miscarriage. We also inform parents-to-be about the ways in which they can reduce the risk of having a problem pregnancy.

What is smalltalk ?

Tommy's Campaign has launched a great new club, called 'smalltalk', for parents with babies and toddlers. All you need to do is pay £2 a month (£24 a year) to join. This money will help fund doctors and scientists nationwide in our vital research into the causes of problems in pregnancy.

Join smalltalk and help save a tiny life

If you join smalltalk, you will receive three magazines a year, packed full of hints, tips and advice on parenting – from early-learning ideas for babies through to coping with toddler tantrums, for example. The magazine also features special

readers' offers and competitions and, on first subscribing, you'll receive a free gift.

In addition, we will report back on all the latest news on Tommy's Campaign research – it's the very least we can do. After all, it's only through your generosity and support that we will be able to continue our work towards giving more babies the best possible start in life.

Remember, for just £2 a month you will:

- receive three free issues a year of *smalltalk* magazine
- receive a free Tiny Love toy when you first join
- benefit from special readers' offers and competitions relating to your favourite parenting products
- help fund vital medical research into the causes of problems in pregnancy.

Call free on 0800 096 0508 with your credit card details to SIGN UP NOW!

Tommy's Campaign

Finding the answers to problem pregnancies

Registred charity number 1060508

Acknowledgments

Dorling Kindersley would like to thank the following:

Editorial and design
Dawn Bates and Caroline Greene for their editorial contributions, and Elly King, Bernhard Koppmeyer, Sally Smallwood and Dawn Young for their design assistance.

Photography
Andy Crawford, Jo Foord, Steve Gorton, Ruth Jenkinson, Dave King, David Murray, Ian O'Leary, Susanna Price, Tim Ridley, Jules Selmes and Steve Shott.

Picture credits
Front cover and swimming picture (idea 98) by kind permission of Mother & Baby Picture Library.

Nursery rhymes
The editors have made every effort to establish the identity of possible copyright holders for the nursery rhymes featured, but the investigations strongly suggest that the rhymes used are in the public domain.